CW00501982

SPIRITUAL MANIFESTATIONS THROUGH THE FIVE PILLARS OF ISLAM

Mohammed Roziur Rahman

ACKNOWLEDGEMENTS

I would like to express my very profound gratitude to my friends and family, especially the late Dr Ataullah Siddiqui of the Markfield Institute of Higher Education, Leicester. The door to Dr Ataullah's office was always open whenever I ran into trouble or had a question about my writing. He consistently helped me shape my ideas to produce benefits in the right direction.

I would like to thank my dear friend Abdurrahman Smith for his help with editing the content of this book.

Finally, I would like to express my gratitude to all of my teachers both in secular and Islamic institutions. Without their passionate dedication towards me, this book would not have been accomplished.

This book is dedicated to my beloved children, Ishaaq, Hannah and Maaria, and my spiritual mentor, the late Shaykh Yusuf Motala.

We are not human beings having a spiritual experience; we are spiritual beings having a human experience.

-Teilhard de Chardin-

PREFACE

For many years I had wanted to write a book on Islam that would appeal to both Muslims and generic audiences alike. Through my roles as Imam, interfaith director and chaplain, I developed various ways of explaining Islam to other people. Some methods were evangelical, some were universal and some were influenced by dogmatic Islamic resources. I always refurbished the wheel of *dawah* (propagating Islam) to befit specific audiences. I felt that I was well-positioned to engage with people in beneficial ways. In a world full of uncertainty and turmoil due to the COVID pandemic starting in 2020, I embraced solitude and silence in a way that I had never done so before. By staying at home and only going outside by myself, I would stare at the sunrise and sunset along the ocean, which caused me to reflect inwardly. It was during Ramadan, at the height of the global pandemic, that I commenced writing every night about Islam and its spiritual manifestations. The book was completed in 3 weeks through passion, dedication and a sense of building a lasting spiritual legacy for myself, my children and the world. Many books have been written on Islam and its foundations, whether they be theological, practical or spiritual. This book aims to dig a bit deeper into the psycho-spiritual reasoning of Islam by exploring that which is commonly known as the five pillars of Islam: the testimony of faith, prayer, charity, fasting and pilgrimage.

I am thankful to God for enabling me to accomplish this work. Everything is achieved according to God's decree, and I feel that this was the right time.

This book can be used as a guide by anyone who wants to focus on the spiritual mapping of the human soul through Islam. Every word in this book is a spiritual legacy that I leave behind for the world to embrace. I hope you can find it within yourself to spread my word, reflect upon it and take up the task of expressing your spirituality throughout life. This will help you navigate towards spiritual wholeness.

Mohammed Roziur Rahman

20th Ramadan 2020

Find yourself in this book, let yourself go and embrace the cosmic origin of your soul through all of God's glory.

INTRODUCTION

What is Islam?

Through faith and loyalty, Islam maintains a connection between humans and God throughout life and death. In addition to this form of allegiance, a treasure of intellectual, moral, and social frameworks is available. These frameworks help cleanse the human heart of negativity and darkness and fill it with positivity and light.

Islam may be described as a faith, a religion, or a tradition, depending on the individual and their spiritual journey towards God. There are different levels of devotional desire among Muslim adherents, and not all of them are on the same spiritual journey.

Islam is manifested through spiritual frameworks, such as prayer, derived from the teachings of the Quran and the traditions of the Prophet Muhammad (peace and blessings be upon him). Muhammad (peace and blessings be upon him) is considered by Islam to be the culmination of God's chosen messengers who include Jesus, Moses and Abraham (peace be upon them all). Muhammad (peace and blessings be upon him) delivered the Quran to mankind as God's universal message. A message of hope, peace, and spiritual purpose.

A major purpose of Islam is to recalibrate humankind towards God to achieve eternal bliss. Islam is essentially a roadmap through life and death. We will briefly discuss the terms used in defining the Islamic tradition in the following sections.

Who is a Muslim?

A Muslim adheres to the above-mentioned interpretation of Islam. In doing so, a Muslim is peaceful at heart and finds comfort in God's remembrance through prayer, patience and gratitude. This source of acquired peace then manifests in the individual's speech, and that of other people and the world in general. As such, a Muslim is at peace with God and God's creation through acts of virtue, compassion and justice.

God or Allah?

In order to appeal to generic audiences of faith and those of no faith, the word God will be used instead of Allah. This is within the Quranic context of godliness. As its primary audience consisted of Arabs, the Quran utilises the word 'Allah' for God.

The utilisation of the word 'God' is arguably contested by some Muslim and Christian theologians[1] due to differences in Christology and Prophetology. This involves whether Jesus is deemed divine or not. One of the most unique chapters in the Quran describes God in the following manner: Say: **"He is Allah, the One! Allah, the Eternal, the Absolute!". "He begets not, nor was He begotten, and there is none comparable unto Him"** (*Al-Ikhlaas* 112: 1-4). This book, therefore, describes God within the Islamic context of godliness, detached from any aspect of the trinity within the Christian tradition, or the gods from other traditions

---

[1] Von Stosch, K. (7). Does Allah Translate 'God'? Translating Concepts between Religions. Translating religion: What is lost and gained, 47, 123.

Why is the Quran in Arabic?

Though Muhammad (peace and blessings be upon him) was born in the Arabian Peninsula in 570 CE[2], the message of Islam is fundamentally universal and not a promotion of Arabism.

The Quran is considered God's final revelation and was revealed in Arabic, the language of Muhammad (peace and blessings be upon him) and his people. There are many reasons for this, but one such explanation is that due to the density and complexity of the Arabic language, the depth of God's message in the Quran could be understood in multiple ways to facilitate a diversity of thought throughout the world. The Quran states in chapter 12, verse 2, **"Lo! We have revealed lectures in Arabic that you may understand"** (*Yusuf* 12: 2).

Besides being an expressive language in terms of personal pronouns, verb inflexions and formation of words, the Arabic language is multi-dimensional with the power and ability to remove misunderstanding and influence semantic shifts.

---

[2] Rogerson, B. 2010

God states in the Quran, chapter 14, verse 4, **"and we never sent a Messenger, except in the language of his nation, that he might make (Our revealed message) clear for them"** (*Ibrahim* 14: 4).

God has revealed scripture to His chosen messengers in the language of their people. For example, the Torah was delivered to Moses in Hebrew, the language spoken and understood by him and his people. Likewise, the Gospel was delivered to Jesus in Greek-Aramaic, the language spoken and understood by him and his people. Similar examples can be found for various other prophets and scriptures. The Quran is portrayed as a universal guide for mankind. It encourages people to learn Arabic to fully immerse themselves in God's spiritual and diverse dominion.

Now that we have explored the terms 'Islam', 'Muslim' and the 'Quran' we can begin to examine the first spiritual pillar of Islam, namely the *Shahada*.

SHAHADA

In Islam, '*Shahada*' is an Arabic term used to define spiritual growth through allegiance to God and the monotheistic traditions of prophets such as Abraham, Moses, Jesus and Muhammad (peace be upon them all). *Shahada* is essentially the fountain of practical Islam; a means to continuously highlight the purpose of life and worldly existence through remembrance of God with gratitude, humility and humanity.

The common mantra used to express belief in God in Islam is 'there is none worthy of worship but Allah and Muhammad is His messenger'. The common Arabic word to define God is 'Allah', as mentioned before. The recognition of Muhammad (peace and blessings be upon him) as God's prophet is to accept the finality of God's divine message to the world through Islam. The *shahada* phenomenon also includes acknowledging previous divine messages that prophets, including Jesus and Moses, received from God.

The Islamic term *'Tawheed'* is the conceptual backbone of Islamic monotheism in the interpretation of the Oneness of God. It essentially defines the theological and practical relationship between humans and God through a spiritual hierarchy; that God is supreme and singular in His ability to reform humans in all aspects of life. The stronger the understanding one attains around *tawheed*, the wider the light of God grows through the *shahada* phenomenon, as discussed later, in every moment of ease and difficulty.

Shahada refers to the idea of witnessing something. In Islam, it is to witness God's light as it substitutes darkness and to become empowered by His spiritual embrace and presence. The more prominent the *shahada* phenomenon in this aspect, the greater the manifestation of internal motivation towards God in one's life.

Spiritual growth in the *Shahada*

Shahada can primarily be interpreted as belief, essentially the activity of the mind. To sustain belief is to be compelled by what is portrayed. Sometimes the outcome of any form of belief can range from adhering to habitual rituals to quite simply having belief without ritual.

In Islam, the impact of sustaining the *shahada* is not only tied to ritual or simple belief but essentially a process of shaping the human from a state of hopelessness to hopefulness in God. This section aims to briefly portray the process of sustaining hope through the *shahada* phenomenon by exploring the relationship between humankind and God.

In Islam, *Shahada* refers to the concept of testifying to the truth of this world and the afterlife. It also highlights human fragility compared to God's Majesty, and in doing so, a state of internal reflection develops through intrigue and exploration of the world and beyond. God states in the Quran, **"And I did not create the *Jinn* and mankind except to worship Me"** (*al-Dhariyat* 51: 56).

The idea of worship is to be in a constant state of spiritual exploration whilst seeking purposeful intent towards God. Therefore, in Islam, *shahada* essentially creates a simultaneous form of internal and external loyalty to God and a state of gratitude and servitude. The concept of gratitude and servitude in Islam, besides appreciating God's gifts throughout life, is to enhance spiritual connection with God through His remembrance habitually.

God states in the Quran, **"Remember me and I will remember you"** (*al-Baqarah* 2: 152). This is a reminder of God's default connection with His creation. God knew His creation before they were born. God loved His creation before they were loved by anyone else. God was always there when no one else was present in the cosmos. Therefore, in God's remembrance, traits of patience, acceptance and ease in the fulfilment of God's decree develop throughout life.

In Islam, the growth and decline of spiritual growth are underpinned by the level of belief, gratitude and patience retained within the heart. This is achieved through hope and fulfilment found in God's remembrance. Hence, maintaining a delicate balance between hope and hopelessness, though hard at times, is deemed a form of spiritual wholeness in Islam.

In Islam, God is considered diverse through His attributes and qualities. He is considered to have 99 qualities known to mankind that are termed '*Asma ul Husna*' or 'the beautiful names of God'. These names are either found in the Quran or Hadith (prophetic narrations of Muhammad (peace and blessings be upon him)). The Prophet Muhammad (peace and blessings be upon him) said: **"There are ninety-nine names of Allah; he who commits them to memory would get into Paradise. Verily, Allah is Odd (He is One, and it is an odd**

number) and He loves an odd number" (Muslim: 5). This Hadith could be understood in the following manner:

a) Committing His names to memory refers to the memory of the human soul. In other words, one should beautify one's heart with the remembrance of God and His attributes.

b) The reference to entry into paradise relates to the paradise of the soul, the world and the hereafter. In other words, when God is the centrepiece of one's consciousness then essentially the soul has tasted paradise, life becomes meaningful, and the afterlife is enhanced by reunion with God through eternal bliss.

c) Lastly, the reference to God as an odd number emphasises the notion that God is One and unique in every way.

God's 99 names and attributes can be appreciated and understood through every shade of colour, life experience, spiritual experience and tradition. God says in the following verses of the Quran: **"To Allah belong the best names, so invoke Him by them"** (*al-A 'raf* 7: 180); **"Allah – there is no deity except Him. To Him belong the best names"** (*Ta Ha* 20: 8); **"He is Allah, the Creator, the Inventor, the Fashioner; to Him belong the best names"** (*al-Ḥashr* 59:

24). Some of the names of God include *Ar-Rahman* (the Most Beneficent), *Ar-Raheem* (the Most Merciful), and *Al-Malik* (the Dominion). Besides these, a full list is given at the end of this book.

One can see through this discussion that *shahada* is to testify to God's creativity and divine diversity. Lack of this acknowledgement potentially stagnates spiritual growth with God throughout life and can cause hopelessness. Within the realm of Islamic spirituality, through the five pillars of Islam, the human soul is essentially the bridge that connects Muslims with God. Nurturing of the human soul is essential for maintaining a connection with God within this worldly realm. The next section explores the concept of the human soul in Islam and further explains this spiritual phenomenon.

The human soul in Islam

In Islam, the human is made up of four elements (Ali, A. 1953); the body, the mind, the soul, and the self. Understanding the concept of the human soul in Islam is integral to the essence of knowing the purpose of spiritual life and spiritual death.

The human soul is called *'Ruh'* in the Arabic language. It is the underlying transient essence of humans. The human soul is difficult to rationally grasp due to it being a mystery of God's divine inspiration. The Quran says: **"And they ask you (Muhammad) about the soul; say, the soul is of the instruction of my Lord. And you have been given little knowledge of it"** (*al-Isra'* 17: 85).

According to Islamic psychologists and theologians (Ashy, M. A, 1999), the *ruh* is a non-materialistic reality that permeates the entire human body, but it is specifically positioned within the human heart, which in Arabic is known as the *'Qalb'*.

Qalb: the human heart

In the Quran, God states that on the Day of Judgement nothing will be of any use to humans except **"a tranquil heart"** (*al-Shu'ara'* 26: 89). The Prophet Muhammad (peace and blessings be upon him) once said: **"Indeed in the body, there is a piece of flesh. If it is tranquil, the entire body is tranquil. If it is corrupt, the entire body is corrupt. Indeed, it is the heart"** (Muslim: 1599).

Concerning this, Islamic scholars throughout the centuries have created spiritual sciences dedicated to exploring various complex traits of the human heart. Spiritual tranquillity is the goal of these sciences. In recent times, the name given to this science is Islamic psychology (Al-Karam, C. Y, 2018), although some would argue that Sufism (Haque, A., Khan, 2016) is a more fitting name in this regard.

In the next section, we explore the connection between the human soul and heart and its connection to the essence of the *shahada* phenomenon.

The connection between the human heart and the soul

Islamic scripture indicates that when living beings are born into the world, the *ruh* (the soul) is pure, full of God's light and in a sound state within the heart. As the human being develops throughout life and becomes influenced by worldly surroundings, the soul becomes agitated. Therefore, it struggles to maintain a spiritual relation with the heart and help it achieve a balance between spirituality and materialism. Without any form of spiritual discipline in this regard, the heart becomes accustomed to worldly distractions and adopts unhealthy attitudes towards the human soul. The human soul then becomes trapped by the rustiness of the heart and struggles to shine through this internal conflict.

Once the heart is maintained through a process of self-discipline and behavioural enhancing environments, then the rustiness of the heart disappears and is enlightened by the light of the soul. The heart is then preserved from negative influences and is recalibrated towards the presence and reality of God. Both the enlightened human soul and heart become entwined through spiritual tranquillity whilst achieving closeness to God. This changing process of the human soul and heart happens every day in our lives. With the right guidance and support, the tranquil state of the heart and soul can be achieved.

In Islam, conforming to rules and rituals may be simple enough for many, but it is only a form of external appreciation of God. The real work of spiritual progress starts from nurturing the soul and heart and is essential for the one aiming to become a human being with a spiritual heart in a troubled world.

Speaking of the heart, a very essential part of spiritual revival is the process of combatting the most stubborn part known as the '*Nafs*' in Arabic. The Quran says: **"As for one that fears standing before their Lord, and forbids the *nafs* of its desires, for them, Heaven shall be his place of abode"** (*al-Nazi'at* 79: 40). Once the *nafs* is spiritually managed, the human soul beams its light towards the heart and infuses it with motivation towards virtuous deeds with ease. Hence, a greater way to maximise the potential benefits of the five spiritual pillars of Islam is to continuously condition the *nafs* to recalibrate the heart towards God.

In the next section, we explore the importance of the *shahada* and reflection concerning humankind in their journey to God.

Shahada and internal reflection

In the previous section, the Islamic perspective on the human soul and heart and their journey to God were explored. In this section, the relationship between the *shahada* phenomenon and human soul and its impact on the heart is analysed through the benefits of self-reflection.

When the heart is in the highest state of God-consciousness due to its regulative nature, *shahada* then becomes the energy flow of God's presence within the human psyche every day. Once a human being gradually realises their potential growth through the *shahada* phenomenon, the irresistible journey to God never ends. Finding God amid chaos is like the light of hope that shines through mist and darkness. In Islam, the path to God is as diverse as are human beings and beyond. Each human being explores various shades of God in ascension to spiritual wholeness.

Shahada is the art of spiritual meditation that draws the human being towards finding a purpose and place in this world. The greater the mastery in developing the art of the *shahada,* the greater the devotion to God and His creation. In Islam, for a Muslim to serve God's creation is to essentially appreciate God's diversifying love for all, respect human boundaries and embrace one's unique identity in the world.

If a Muslim is devoid of any form of reflective process and discipline, a contradiction develops between the purpose of spiritual growth and committing rituals towards God. In Islam, rituals performed without any desire to enhance internal spiritual growth stagnates the development of potential human wisdom and noble character. Human life would be lacking direction and value if the foundations of *shahada* are not fulfilled cohesively with the heart and soul. One can therefore become susceptible to demoralisation and moral stagnation.

In the next section, an exploration of the *shahada* phenomenon through a set of spiritual beliefs takes place. This is to enhance understanding of what it means to witness God through the spiritual heart in the world today.

The foundations of the *shahada*

This section refers to a set of spiritual themes or beliefs that support one's journey towards acknowledging God through life and beyond. Some of these themes are like other faith traditions and some are exclusive to Islam. In the Quran, reference is made to having belief and conviction in unseen matters as the hallmark of being a Muslim. God states in the Quran: **"O you who believe! Keep faith in Allah and His Messenger and the Book which He revealed to His Messenger, and the Book which He revealed before. Whoever disbelieves in Allah, His angels, His Books, and His Messengers and the Last Day, has verily wandered far astray"** (*al-Nisa'* 4: 136). These themes of belief are collectively known as the articles of Islamic faith or '*Iman*'. Muslim theologians have established these themes as the foundations of Islamic belief. The purpose of this theological establishment in Islam is to encourage humankind to make sense of this world through the lens of Islam and its mystical tradition.

The six articles of faith are belief in God, angels, divine books, God's messengers, destiny, the Day of Judgement, and life after death. We have explored the concept of God already within this chapter and now the remaining articles of belief will be outlined.

a) Acknowledging angels

There are many interpretations related to their creation, relevance and place in common culture. In Islam, they are considered a unique creation of God, designed to carry out His various commands. As they are not gendered, caste, or colour bound, they have many wings attached to their bodies. God created angels out of spiritual light known as '*Nur*' in Arabic. Aishah (may Allah be pleased with her) reported: **"The Messenger of Allah (peace and blessings be upon him) said: "The angels are created from light, just as the *Jinn***

are created from smokeless fire, and mankind is created from what you have been informed" (Muslim).

The *Jinn* are beings created by God with free will, residing on earth in a space like humankind. The Arabic term *jinn* is from the verb '*Janna*' which means to be concealed. Therefore, the *jinns* are invisible from humankind.

Regarding angels, the Quran has a whole chapter entitled 'Angels' that speaks of their creation. God states: **"Praise be to Allah, Who fashioned (out of nothing) the heavens and the earth, Who made the angels messengers with wings - two, or three, or four (pairs) and adds to creation as He pleases: for Allah has power over all things"** (*Fatir* 35:1).

According to Islamic scripture, the number of angels is unknown. But what is known is that they patrol the heavens and the earth to indicate God's love and majesty to mankind. Angels are an investment of God for mankind so that people feel secure and know His presence, even during times of loneliness. Amongst all types of environments, angels thrive in places where God is remembered.

Abu Hurayrah (may Allah be pleased with him) stated: **"The Messenger of Allah (peace and blessings of Allah be upon Him) said: "Allah, be He blessed and exalted, has angels** who travel the highways seeking out the people of *dhikr* (remembrance). When they find people remembering Allah, the Mighty and Majestic, they call out to one another, "Come to what you hunger for!" and they enfold them with their wings, stretching up to the lowest heaven. Their Lord asks them, and He knows better than them, "What are my slaves saying?" They reply: "They are glorifying, magnifying, praising and extolling You." He asks, "Have they seen Me?" They reply, "No, by Allah, they have not seen You." He asks, "And how would it be if they saw Me?" They say, "They would be even more fervent and devoted in their praise and worship." He asks, "What are they asking Me for?" They say, "They ask You for Paradise." He asks, "And have they seen it?" They say, "No, by Allah, O Lord, they have not seen it." He asks, "And how would it be if they saw it?" They say: "They would be even more eager for it, and they would beseech You even more earnestly." He asks, "And what do they seek My protection from?" They respond, "From the Fire of Hell." He asks, "Have they seen it?" They respond, "No, by Allah, they have not seen it." He asks, "And how would it be if they saw it?" They replied: "They would be even more afraid and anxious to escape it." Allah says: "You are my witnesses that I have forgiven them." One of the angels says: "So-and-so is not one of them; he came (to the gathering) for some other reason." Allah says, "They were all in the gathering, and one of them will not be excluded (from forgiveness)" (Bukhari: 6408[3]).

It can be understood from this narration the importance of spiritual attachment to God. Secondly, the presence of angels is deemed more noteworthy whilst God is being remembered. This indicates that remembering God is key to embracing the company of angels and vice versa. This should, therefore, provide solace and comfort for the distressed and lonely.

b) Acknowledging divine scriptures

The Quran mentions the names of some scriptures that were sent to various messengers of God. Those that are mentioned include the Psalms, Torah and Gospel. God states in the Quran the following verses:

"Indeed, We have entrusted Our Messengers with clear proofs and revealed with them the Scripture and the Balance (justice) that mankind may keep up justice" (*al-Hadid* 57: 25). **"We sent Jesus, son of Mary, in their**

---

[3] Sahih Bukhari is a collection of sayings and deeds of Prophet Muhammad, also known as the Sunnah. Khan, M. M. (1986).

footsteps, to confirm the Torah that had been sent before him: We gave him the Gospel with guidance, light, and confirmation of the Torah already revealed – a guide and lesson for those who take heed of God … We sent to you [Muhammad] the Scripture with the truth, confirming the Scriptures that came before it, and with final authority over them" (*al-Ma'idah* 5: 46- 48).

"**And to David, we granted the Zaboor (Psalms)**" (*al-Ma'idah* 4: 163).

"**Verily, We did send down the Torah [to Musa], therein was guidance and light, by which the Prophets, who submitted themselves to Allah's Will, judged the Jews. Likewise, the scholars and rabbis judged the Jews by the Torah after those Prophets, since they were entrusted with the responsibility of protecting Allah's Book. They were witnesses thereto. Therefore, fear not men but fear Me (O Jews) and sell not My Verses for a miserable price. And whosoever does not judge by what Allah has revealed, such are the disbelievers**" (*al-Ma'idah* 5: 44).

Besides these books, there were other manuals given to many other prophets, such as Abraham and his offspring. God states in the Quran: "**Say (O Muslims): We believe in Allah and**

that which has been sent down to us and that which has been sent down to Ibrahim, Isma'il, Ishaq, Y'aqub, and to Al-Asbat [the offspring of the twelve sons of Y'aqub], and that which has been given to Musa and 'Isa, and that which has been revealed to the prophets from their Lord. We make no distinction between any of them, and to Him, we have submitted (in Islam)" (*al-Baqarah* 2: 136).

The purpose of acknowledging divine scriptures is to identify and appreciate God's compassion and guidance to the world. This means exploring and understanding God's centrality throughout scripture so that His Oneness is felt as unique by all. The Quran promotes a form of religious pluralism that enhances the notion that God's spiritual light shines throughout infinite time and scripture.

For some Muslims, religious pluralism may be a contested issue. Some could argue that religious pluralism is a key component in striving towards the understanding of God's light through robust dialogue. The universal nature of the Quran as God's final message to mankind, as understood by Muslims, is to connect with God's divine presence as a beacon and hope for mankind.

Understanding the various shades of God's divine light through understanding divine scripture can enable social cohesion and compatibility amongst seekers of God's love. This can enable a sense of spiritual companionship to develop through mutual understanding and love.

The love of God is unbridled for all people, whether they see His light or not. God's light is ever-present for those that wish to infuse their hearts with spiritual ascendency. Being a Muslim in this manner is a means to increase one's level of *shahada* through witnessing God's shades of love through people regardless of background.

c) Acknowledging God's messengers

Like acknowledging God's scriptures, His chosen messengers have also portrayed forms of religious and spiritual pluralism that promote God's creation as one spiritual family. The Quran mentions that a messenger was sent to every nation and that some are known, and some are not. God states in the Quran: **"Verily, We have inspired you (O Muhammad) as We inspired Noah and the Prophets after him; We inspired Abraham, Ismail, Isaac, Jacob, and Al-Asbat (the twelve sons of Jacob), Jesus, Job, Jonah, Aaron, Solomon, and to David We granted the Zaboor (Psalms). And there**

are previous Messengers We have mentioned to you, and some We have not named, and to Moses, Allah spoke directly" (*al-Nisa'* 4: 163-164).

The Prophet Muhammad (peace and blessings be upon him) is considered by Muslims to be God's final messenger according to the Quran, and that he was sent as a 'mercy to the worlds', referring to both the physical and spiritual domains of this world and the hereafter. In other words, the Prophet Muhammad (peace and blessings be upon him) was sent as a guide towards spiritual purification of the heart and material regulation considering God's pleasure and guidance.

By understanding Islam through modes of religious pluralism in this manner, one can appreciate the universality of God through scripture, messengers and divine guidance. The theme of spiritual universality in Islam is crucial to the growth of *shahada* in ascendancy to God through the love of His creation.

d) Acknowledging the Day of Judgement

In Islam, the concept of judgement and assessment before God is believed to be a physical reality in the hereafter. Spiritual assessment takes place once the finite universe comes to a halt by God's decree. God's infinity will become apparent to all resurrected humans. The Day of Judgement in Islam is the assessment of human souls, through their journey of life from birth to death. In the Quran, many verses speak of the Day of Judgement. The following verses are some descriptions:

"Did you then think that We had created you in jest (without any purpose) and that you would not be returned to Us (in the Hereafter)? So, God is exalted, the True King. None has the right to be worshipped but Him" (*al-Mu'minun* 23: 115-116).

"But when there comes the Deafening Blast - that Day a man will flee from his brother, and his mother and his father, and his wife and his children. For each one of them, that day will have enough preoccupations of his own. Some faces, that day, will be bright – laughing, rejoicing at the good news. And other faces, that Day, will have upon them dust. Darkness will cover them. Those are the disbelievers (in God), the wicked ones" (*'Abasa* 80: 33-42).

Disbelief in Islam refers to denying God and His presence as the Lord of both worlds. The term *'Kafir'* is used to describe this in Arabic, although 'ungratefulness to God' is also an understanding of this word, theologically speaking. The difference between a Muslim and a *Kafir* lies in having gratitude to God. A Muslim is grateful to God whereas a *Kafir* is considered the opposite.

Muslims are motivated by the reality of afterlife to revive their soul and heart with spiritual discipline towards God throughout life. Life is therefore considered a way of preparing the human soul for its reunion with God in the best possible state of spirituality.

Death is considered a door to the afterlife, to be reunited with God in bliss and serenity. Concerning positive and negative deeds, God states: **"On that day, people will come forward in separate groups to be shown their deeds: whoever has done an atom's weight of good will see it, but whoever has done an atom's weight of evil will see that"** (*al-Zalzalah* 99: 6-8).

The Prophet Muhammad (peace and blessings be upon him) emphasised that **"God does not observe what wealth or beauty one possesses but the state of the human heart and worldly deeds"** (Muslim: 2564). The assessment of every intention and action in the hereafter is based upon the merit of one's worldly motivation. Hence, habitually reviving one's spiritual motivation in life is a key component to driving the heart towards spiritual wholeness. This could, therefore, provide mental and behavioural regulation during day-to-day activities and a sense of renewed purpose. This results in the *shahada* phenomenon growing, maturing and providing purposefulness in life.

e) Acknowledging fate

Fate in Arabic is referred to as *'Qadr'* or *'Taqdeer'*. In Islam, fate is deemed to be God's decree for all creation. Those that possess a free will to act, such as human beings, dictate their lives within the realm of God's knowledge. God states in the Quran: **"And with Him are the keys of the unseen; none knows them except Him. And He knows what is on the land and in the sea. Not a leaf falls without His knowledge. And no grain is there within the darkness of the earth and no moist or dry [thing] but that it is [written] in a clear record"** (*al-An'am* 6: 59).

God is considered diverse and mysterious in His decree for His creation and so, this Quranic verse highlights the complexities around understanding fate among humans.

Ali narrated that one day the Messenger of Allah (peace and blessings be upon him) was sitting with a wooden stick in his hand with which he was scratching the ground. As he raised his head, he said, **"None one of you has a place assigned to him except in the Fire or Paradise." They (the Companions) inquired, "O Allah's Messenger! "Why should we carry on doing righteous deeds, shall we depend (upon *Qadr*) and give up work?" He said: "No, carry on doing virtuous deeds, for everyone will find it easy (to do) such deeds that will lead him towards that for which he has been created." Then he recited the Quranic verse** (*al-Lail* 92:5-7) : **"As for him who gives (in charity) and keeps his duty to Allah and fears Him, and believes in al-Husna, We will make smooth for him the path of ease (goodness)"** (Muslim, 6398).

In Islam, particular acts bring about positive change within one's decree. For example, being kind to people is considered a way of being kind yourself. Through this, one's fate is shaped by positive will and action. God states in the Quran: **"Allah never changes the condition of people until they strive to change themselves"** (*al-Ra'd* 13: 11).

God is considered by Muslims to be the causation of executing good and determination towards spiritual consciousness in life. Muslims find solace in God's decree throughout life whilst increasing the *shahada* phenomenon.

The idea of *qadr* is not to do nothing and wait for God's decree, due to His knowledge of the unseen, but to use one's will as a means of spreading positivity in the world. Doing so enables the human being to become enlightened by the light of God through the highs and lows of life.

f) Acknowledging life after death

The Islamic idea that the human soul is transient is commonly understood through the concept of life and death. After death, the human soul visits God for a brief assessment. The soul is then returned to its body in the grave to rest until the Day of Judgement.

Within the grave, according to Islamic scripture, the human soul either remains at ease or in a state of anxiety, due to the result of God's assessment. Death is considered the portal to the eternal resting place of the soul. In Islam, securing one's place of eternal bliss in the hereafter is considered a reflection of a virtuous and noble life. God states in the Quran: **"Indeed, Allah [alone] has knowledge of the Hour and sends down the rain and knows what is in the wombs. And no soul perceives what it will earn tomorrow, and no soul perceives in what land it will die. Indeed, Allah is Knowing and Acquainted"** (*Luqman* 31: 34).

In the state of suspension between death and resurrection, the human soul acknowledges its permanent abode in the hereafter through the visualisation of Heaven or Hell in the grave, unseen to human beings.

For Muslims, knowing of the afterlife causes motivation towards positivity, rituals and retaining God-consciousness in life. According to the Quran, **"Everyone will taste death. You will be paid your wages in full on the Day of Rising. Anyone who is distanced from the Fire and admitted to the Garden has triumphed. The life of this world is only the enjoyment of delusion"** (*al 'Imran* 3: 185). Here, God reminds humankind that its shared destiny is death and that no one can escape it. The Quran reminds humankind to not take life for granted and underestimate the gift of time on earth. Despite normative fears many people have of death, for some, embracing the reality of death is the only source of comfort in this world when returning to God in a state of spiritual purity and enlightenment. The more significant the *shahada* phenomenon within one's life, the more meaningful health and illness becomes considering death.

The six articles of *Iman*, or 'faith', are the foundations of *shahada* and provide a divine roadmap for the human being. The human being, in acknowledging the matters of the unseen, begins to reflect and ponder upon the purpose of oneself and life in general. Each creation of God, whether animate or inanimate, has been granted a spiritual presence through God's decree. Human beings can either decide between retaining positive or negative energy through spiritual exploration and reflection in life. That is why meditation within *shahada* is crucial in the development of the human being towards holistic spirituality.

In the next section, the discussion of the *shahada* continues by exploring the benefits of exploration and self-purification.

Exploring God through the lens of the *shahada* and spirituality

In Islam, a lack of development within one's character is due to a lack of divine light within the heart due to an irregular connection with God. When *shahada* is processed in the right manner, as described in previous sections, it will no doubt become a constant healing factor for the human being throughout the journey of life. *Shahada* provides, therefore, a direction and meaning in relationships with human beings, animals and the environment as God's creation on earth.

Shahada is a personal bridge to God. That bridge is personal to each human being and should not be used to define people in unhelpful ways. For example, when someone becomes a Muslim, they enter a realm of spirituality that is defined following one's spiritual needs. To categorise the *shahada* phenomenon according to specific cultural and religious labels in creating an agenda of sectarian dominance, is against the spiritual nature of Islam. *Shahada* is indeed tied to God's universal love, and anything which contradicts it denies the pre-planned connection God has with mankind from the very beginning.

It is an integral part of the Muslim tradition to observe, study and understand various forms of spirituality. Identity is shaped by experiences, and it is imperative to know that each religious tradition within Islam holds multiple interpretations of moral development for the human soul. To allow positive differences to form through healthy dialogue and interaction, one must keep their spiritual identity while acknowledging others. *Shahada* in this manner is considered a form of making sense of spiritual identity, belonging and purpose. If one loses understanding of spiritual identities, held in different ways by different people, then the potential for one's character to become poisoned by tropes of religious supremacy can happen.

Concerning identity and the search for spiritual meaning in Islam, the following section will explore *shahada* in practice.

Shahada in practice

Knowing God is to allow clarity to develop through one's spiritual identity, intentions and actions in life. The greater the clarity, the greater the outcome in achieving purposeful endings with God in the hereafter. By *shahada*, one seeks to maintain one's spiritual identity and to know God. This requires a daily routine to further the benefits of intentionality, clarity, and positive outcomes. In Islam, an act holds virtue at the level of purposeful intent. If one is to maximise the benefit of *shahada* with regards to spiritual growth, then it is paramount to create a constant state of intent whilst moving forward.

For Muslims, the recital of spiritual mantras eradicates the notion of *Shirk,* or 'ascribing partners to God'. *Shirk* is considered the opposite of *shahada*. *Shahada* is focused on the Oneness of God. Shirk is the ascription of God as having attributes of His creation and vice versa, hence, lacking any form of divine uniqueness and diminishing the notion of *tawheed*.

The externalisation of *shahada* through life reflects the language of the human soul in its connection to God. Therefore, Muslims apply the practice of *shahada* in different contexts. For example, the recital of the *shahada* is carried out verbally to facilitate religious needs, such as conversion to Islam. Conversion to Islam reflects a motivated state of mind, body and heart towards a spiritual goal. Thus, embracing Islam is considered a means of reorienting the human being towards the realm of God's light.

Muslims of all backgrounds maintain a connection with God in various ways. Some Muslims are inclined to Islam due to cultural upbringing and family tradition. Rather than adhering to cultural traditions, some Muslims are attracted to Islam through religious rituals. And some Muslims are spiritually inclined to Islam due to life-changing occurrences and internal exploration. Each connection is then interpreted in different ways to suit the individual through belief, practice and outlook. This is sometimes shaped by their experiences in life, the company of people and solitude.

In conclusion, we now see that the *shahada* phenomenon is more than a few words of affirmation to God's call, but an endless journey to Him within a spiritual dimension. This is so that one can develop a practical relationship with God. A dogmatic approach to *shahada* without spiritual awareness and purification of the soul can result in a dogmatic approach to addressing God and His creation. This type of approach can create stagnation towards personal fulfilment, cause disorder within the human experience and harden the heart instead of softening it towards God and His creation. Therefore, for some Muslims, religious rituals can cause a beneficial increase in the sacred nature of the *shahada* and for some, religious rituals have no impact on improving spirituality in *shahada* due to lack of improved character.

The highest form of *shahada* in Islam

The highest form of *shahada* in Islam is known as '*Ihsan*'. *Ihsan,* as described by the Prophet Muhammad (peace and blessings be upon him) is to **"serve God as though you see Him, though you cannot then know He is observing you"** (Abu Dawood: 4695).

What does this mean? During the process of purifying the heart of ill traits, the soul beams the love of God within thought, touch and perception. Therefore, the Prophet Muhammad (peace and blessings be upon him) once explained that the soundness of the human heart causes everything else to remain sound and content. But if the heart is corrupt or susceptible to negativity, then everything else remains negative.

With this point, it is imperative to address the benefit of good company in maintaining a positive mindset in life. Having good company illuminates internal growth and nurtures one to have a positive impact on the world. Hence, maintaining favourable company in life is imperative where possible to ensure spiritual growth within the realm of *shahada*.

The goal of the *Shahada* phenomenon is to enlighten the seeker of God and awaken them to the true nature of His reality. *Shahada* should not, therefore, be reduced to a mere technique of verbalising the Islamic faith but rather a means towards exploring the meaning of life. In doing so, the following benefits are perceived:

a) Mindfulness of God is realised through scrupulousness and uprightness.

b) Adherence to the tradition of the Prophet Muhammad (peace and blessing be upon him) is realised through caution and excellent character.

c) Contentment is achieved through acceptance of what one is given and turning over the management of one's affairs to God.

d) The process of turning back to God grows through habitual praise and gratitude in times of prosperity.

e) Taking refuge in Him in times of affliction.

To conclude, the growth of *shahada* stems from the window of the human heart, namely the soul. Once the heart sees light through this window via spiritual discipline, it becomes prepared to nurture human intrigue and exploration. The greater the light of the soul in the heart, the more jubilant the Muslim becomes when recalibrating to God. This is the impact of *shahada:* a healing foundation for humankind.

In the next chapter, we explore the concept of prayer, known in Arabic as '*Salah*'. We will explore the spiritual dimensions of prayer like we have examined *shahada* in this chapter.

SALAH

We now move on from understanding
the *shahada* phenomenon to exploring the remaining pillars of
Islam, dominated by rituals. These rituals are spiritually
beneficial with increased levels of *shahada*. A constant,
mindful notion of God through ritual practice in Islam
increases the connection between each prayer, fast and
charitable act and leads to spiritual intent and outcome. By
exploring the forthcoming topics, one will come to understand
the practical benefits of each ritual in attaining higher levels
of God-consciousness. One will also come to know how
spiritual depravity in each ritual occurs due to loss of focus,
lack of intention and lower levels of God-consciousness.

What is *Salah*?

Salah is a constant state of humility within the mind, body and
soul through expressions of gratitude to God. *Salah* is not
simply a set of prayers but a series of mindfulness
opportunities that serve to remind one of God's presence, five

times a day. *Salah* is considered the most significant part of a Muslim's daily routine besides *shahada*. *Salah* is the hallmark of Muslim identity and serves as a constant reminder of God's omnipresence in life.

The Quran states: **"Righteousness is not that you turn your faces toward the east or the west, but [true] righteousness is [in] one who believes in Allah, the Last Day, the angels, the Book, and the prophets, and gives wealth, despite a love for it, to relatives, orphans, the needy, the traveller, those who ask [for help], and for freeing slaves; [and who] establishes prayer and gives** *zakah* **(monetary charity); [those who] fulfil their promise when they promise; and [those who] are patient in poverty and hardship and during battle. "Those are the ones who have been true, and it is those who are righteous"** (*al-Baqarah* 2: 177). This verse provides a set of principles around the idea of righteousness in Islam. In addition to charity and other noble character traits, *salah* is an integral part of achieving piety. There are more than sixty-seven verses in the Quran that highlight the importance of *salah* in various ways, some of which will be explored in this chapter.

Before performing *salah* five times a day, Muslims are required to perform a cleansing ritual called *Wudu*. This refers to ablution with clean water or dry earth in the case of one having no water or an illness that prevents water usage. The purpose of ablution is to externally cleanse the body before entering a state of internal purification through prayer. Ablution is also a means to relax the body by freshening one's senses to feel soothed in prayer.

In ablution, there are four main areas of washing: the hair, face, arms and feet. Regarding this, the Quran states: **"Oh you who have believed, when you rise to [perform] prayer, wash your faces and your forearms to the elbows and wipe over your heads and wash your feet to the ankles. Allah does not intend to make difficulty for you, but He intends to purify you and complete His favour upon you that you may be grateful"** (*al-Ma'idah* 5: 6). Washing each of these parts reminds the individual of the bodily gifts given by God. It also reminds the individual of the purpose of having a body, namely, to attain spiritual wholeness. A person's body is an object of trust given by God for safekeeping and doing good. Being healthy is also necessary to retain the gift of life. Therefore, one must eat and drink sufficiently so that energy is maintained for worship.

In addition to the beneficial aspects of *wudu* as explained so far in this chapter, the Islamic understanding of being sinless and pure also holds during *wudu*. Uthman ibn Affan (may Allah be pleased with him) reported that once the Messenger of Allah (peace and blessings be upon him) said: **"He who performed ablution well, his sins would come out of his body, even coming out from under his nails"** (Muslim: 224).

In Islam, washing each bodily part three times during ablution is to be submerged into a state of God-consciousness through repetition and preparation. Therefore, it is not commended to talk whilst performing ablution, as it deters the individual from receiving the blessings of *wudu*. *Wudu* is an integral part of prayer preparation that illuminates the path to worshipping God. In Islam, purification is considered half of one's faith. This means that as much as internal spiritual purification is essential to spiritual growth, maintaining bodily purification is essential too.

Prayer and character development

Moving on from ablution and cleanliness, we will now delve into the spiritual effects of prayer through the lens of the Quran and Muslim tradition. God Almighty states in the Quran: **"Indeed prayer removes ill character and vice, and**

the remembrance of Allah is the greatest" (*al-'Ankabut* 29: 49). This verse portrays the benefits of prayer as being linked to character development and mindfulness of God. The effect of prayer is such that it internally enhances the individual through purity of the soul and imbues positive character. The notion of prayer removing ill-character and vice refers to the lack of desire towards polluting the human heart with negative thoughts. Equally, the remembrance of God also begins to increase one's desire towards having positive thoughts and energy.

This verse serves to portray the benefits of prayer, namely character development and mindfulness of God when performed with the right spiritual intent. It is therefore imperative, before each prayer, to reflect upon one's expected spiritual outcomes, purpose and how it will be achieved. Reflecting before each prayer productively regulates one's thinking.

As mentioned in the previous chapter regarding *shahada*, a constant state of mindfulness of God becomes part of one's consciousness when it is repetitive. Conducting five daily prayers is a means to enhancing the *shahada* phenomenon, in addition to character reformation. Reducing the amount of prayer performed due to negligence can cause one to lose focus on God. It deprives the soul of positivity and leads to hopelessness and anxiety within the mind. The Quran states: **"Indeed, mankind was created anxious: When evil afflicts him, he is impatient, and when good comes to him, he is withholding [of it], except for the observers of prayer – those who are constant in their prayer"** (*al-Ma'arij* 70: 19-23). This verse depicts the normative state of the human condition: anxious and in discomfort. It highlights the benefits of *salah* in creating a balance within the mind, body and soul between difficulties and comfort. This is to ensure that nothing is taken for granted and to hold each period of comfort and difficulty with full value, learning and wisdom.

The five daily prayers are meditation points throughout the day and night that help to keep one's soul in check. The Quran states: **"So establish the Prayer after the decline of the sun (from its zenith, for *Zohr* and then *Asr*) to the dusk of the night (*Maghrib* and then '*Isha*) and the (Quranic) recitation of *Fajr* [prayer]. Indeed, the (Quranic) recitation of *fajr* is witnessed"** (*al-Isra'* 17: 78).

The five daily prayers are further explained in more detail:

Fajr - This is the first prayer of the day and takes place at dawn. It is the shortest prayer of the day and its timing throughout the year is based upon the time of dawn throughout the summer and winter seasons. The beauty of this prayer is that it happens when the mind feels fresh and clear. It enables intense reflection for the day ahead and inculcates immense spiritual benefit for daily planning, motivation and time management. The Prophet Muhammad (peace and blessings be upon him) said: "**Whoever offers the Morning Prayer, he is under the protection of Allah, the Mighty and Sublime"** (Ibn Majah: 3946). This reinforces the notion that God is omnipresent and that His care and knowledge supersedes all else in every way. It also provides comfort before the start of the day in knowing that God's decree is shaped by our free will. This is because using our will for goodness creates blessings in life.

Another interesting point regarding *fajr* prayer is the presence of angels during that time. The Prophet Muhammad (peace and blessings be upon him) said: **"Angels come to you in succession by night and day, and they meet at *fajr* and *asr* prayer. Then those who spent the night among you ascend, and He (Allah) will ask them, although He knows best: 'In what condition did you leave My slaves?' They will say: "We left them when they were praying, and we came to them when they were**

praying" (Bukhari: 555). Angels are representatives of God's mercy on earth. This prayer provides an opportunity for one to be mentioned by angels to God when engaging in His remembrance. These forms of spiritual benefit encourage Muslims to pray, even though it may be in the early hours of the morning.

Zohr - This is the second prayer of the day and occurs during the first part of the afternoon. This is the second-longest prayer of the day and serves to remind the individual of God's presence, as a buffer during work, for instance, to reignite spiritual purpose and dedication throughout the day.

The Prophet Muhammad (peace and blessings be upon him) said regarding the *zohr* prayer: **"This is an hour at which the gates of heaven are opened, and I like that my righteous deeds should rise to heaven at that time"** (**Tirmidhi:** 478). It is understood from this statement that *zohr* is a time when everyone's righteous deeds are reviewed by God. Therefore, praying during this time presents an opportunity for one to be considered by God for entry into heaven. During this time, any work or routine should be paused for one to remember God. Doing this will enable the human soul to become rejuvenated for the rest of the day.

Asr - This is the third prayer of the day and the second shortest prayer. It occurs during the latter part of the afternoon until sunset. This prayer, again, is a reminder of God's presence and can also be deemed a means to assess one's dedication to God while one is engaged in daily chores. Like the virtues of *fajr* and the presence of angels at that time, regarding *asr*, the Prophet Muhammad (peace and blessings be upon him) said:

"He who observes Al-Bardan (*Fajr* and *Asr* prayers) will enter Jannah" (Bukhari: 1047). The term '*al-Bardan*' refers to the cooler periods of the day when the heat or light of the sun starts to dissipate. Some may feel tired during this time or preoccupied with work. Therefore, this prayer is a means of reawakening Muslims towards God.

Magrib - This is the fourth prayer of the day and occurs after sunset. It is one of two nightly prayers that remind one of God's presence. It enables one to reflect on the day, assess one's progress and carry out other spiritual acts such as reciting the Quran.

The Prophet Muhammad (peace and blessings be upon him) said: **"The prayer most favoured by Allah is the *magrib* prayer and one who prays two more units of** prayer after it, Allah will build a house for him in Paradise where he will dwell and find comfort" (Mu'jam Al-Awsat: 6445). God's favouring of this prayer is meant to encourage Muslims to recognise special moments of spiritual attainment throughout the day and night. The period of *magrib* does not last long, as it occurs only until the end of sunset. Therefore, Muslims are encouraged to perform this prayer as soon as possible and to avoid delay.

Esha - This is the final prayer of the day and occurs during the night before one retires to bed. This prayer enables one to fully assess their day, create meaningful spiritual goals and take stock of one's spiritual journey. It enables one to glorify God with thankfulness for the day and the ability to pray. It also creates a special bond with God and builds spiritual motivation for the forthcoming day.

The Prophet Muhammad (peace and blessings be upon him) said: **"Whoever offers *esha* prayer in congregation, it is as though he spent half the night in worship. And whoever offers *fajr* prayer in congregation, it is as though he spent the entire night in worship"** (Muslim: 656). The spiritual benefit of completing this prayer is equivalent to dedicating half a night to worshiping God. In Islam, many acts of minimal effort provide immense spiritual benefit. In this case, just 15 to 20 minutes of prayer are as virtuous as praising God for many hours.

The coolness of the soul through prayer

The Prophet Muhammad (peace and blessings be upon him) used to describe prayer as the coolness of his eyes. He said: **"The coolness of my eyes lies in *salah* (prayer)"** (An-Nasa'I: 3939). He found the comfort of his soul within prayer and hence, it became a blessing for him rather than a burden. The calmness he attained during prayer also resulted in others remaining calm in his company. The calmness attained through prayer does indeed manifest through one's speech and actions and so it becomes a blessing for people rather than a burden. That is the essence of the heart when it is purified and sweetened through the grace of God in prayer.

Furthermore, the benefits of congregational prayer within the Islamic tradition outweigh individualised prayer because of the benefits it creates for communities. Such as building communal peace and unity, diversity and inclusion, belonging and purposefulness, and peace and stability.

In addition to the performance of ablution before prayer as mentioned before, the following conditions are also essential when preparing for prayer:

a) To maintain the direction of prayer to Mecca to be mindful of God's omnipresence.

b) To maintain the cleanliness of the body and clothing to increase mindfulness of one's physical state.

c) To maintain clarity of intention in a conscious state for prayer.

d) To maintain locational cleanliness in one's surroundings and environment and to avoid disturbance.

e) To perform prayer on time to ensure better regulation of time management throughout the day and night.

Praying is not viewed as a duty to God but as a service to one's spiritual growth. If one maintains an intrigued mindset towards prayer, then it will not be deemed burdensome long-term. Moving away from a dogmatic approach to prayer towards a more reflective embrace ensures that prayer becomes a means of spiritual nourishment for the heart.

Everyone's outcome of prayer will reflect their preparation, state of intention, direction and expectation. Each purposeful intention, direction and expectation, therefore, facilitates spiritual growth and the productive use of time.

Concerning the gift of time, God states in the Quran: **"By the time, indeed mankind is in loss, except for those who have believed and done righteous deeds and advised each other to truth and advised each other to patience"** (*al-'Asr* 103:1-3). Time is considered God's spiritual blessing for all and beautifully manifests through one's determination to grow spiritually throughout life. The Prophet Muhammad (peace and blessing be upon him) said: **"There are two blessings which many people lose: (They are) health and free time for doing well"** (Bukhari: 6049). From this statement, Muslims should ensure that their lives revolve around better use of time through prayer, reflection and rituals. Furthermore, the Prophet Muhammad (peace and blessing be upon him) said: **"Take advantage of five matters before five other matters: your youth before you become old; your health, before you fall sick; your wealth, before you become poor; your free time before you become preoccupied, and your life, before your death"** (Shu'abul Iman: 9575).

The blessedness of time serves the importance of rituals in Islam and ensures that Muslims are conscious of their prayers. Rituals in Islam provide immense light in a world full of darkness and despair, hence prayer is considered a source of light that removes sadness and provides comfort.

The Prophet Muhammad (peace and blessings be upon him) described prayer saying: **"*Salah* is a light"** (Muslim: 223). The Arabic term used for light in this context is '*Noor*'. *Noor* provides direction, focus and determination through the chaos of life via attachment to God. Therefore, the prophets of old, such as Jesus and Moses, were habitual in prayer; so that they could return to their peoples with God's light and merciful embrace.

Physical motions during prayer

We will now look at the motions of prayer and their spiritual benefits. During the beginning phase of each prayer, Muslims raise both hands towards the ears with palms facing forwards. They then place them on the chest or below the navel whilst reciting *Allahu Akbar*, meaning God is mighty. This movement symbolises the removal of worldly thoughts, pushing them behind whilst entering God's spiritual court.

The next phase of prayer is the bowing position, which is done by slightly bending one's back in a forward motion. This position essentially lowers the human ego into a state of humility before God. It also strengthens the heart by submitting to the will of God and His decree.

Within prayer, the bowing motion is considered a means of regulating the *nafs*. The *nafs* has various levels of perfected and imperfect states according to the level of one's conditioning of their soul. No person is flawless, but the right level of self-discipline can reduce gravitation towards negative influences. Regarding prayer, it allows the soul to connect with the *nafs* and thus illuminates the path to God in the most radiant way possible.

Once the bowing phase is complete, one stands up straight in preparation for prostration. The spiritual benefit from this movement is a renewed direction to God. It can now be considered that the *nafs* has now become conditioned by humility and bowing.

After the standing position, the next phase begins, which is the position of prostration. This happens by lowering one's body to the ground until the head, nose, palms, knees and feet touch the ground, like a yoga position called the 'child's pose'.

Like bowing, prostration suppresses the ego of the individual and therefore conditions the heart intensely. If one considers bowing as a means of causing the heart to be cleansed of darkness and feel raw, then one should know that prostration cools and conditions the heart with God's grace and love. Prostration, known as *Sujood* in Islam, is considered the closest position one can attain with God during prayers.

The last phase of prayer after prostration is to sit down with the hands placed on the thighs, similar to the 'heroes pose' in yoga. During this moment, Muslims supplicate to God and recite blessings upon all angels and prophets of God. By now, the soul will feel refreshed, full of light and calm. Once this phase has been completed, the head is then turned towards the right shoulder. Then it is turned towards the left shoulder whilst reciting words of peace, known in Islam as *Salam*. This movement signifies the end of one's spiritual journey within the prayer. It began with the removal of worldly thoughts before entering God's presence. Then whilst in prayer, the soul passed through a series of purification positions that cleansed the heart and conditioned it with God's love.

In completing the prayer with words of peace, an expression of gratitude to God is made for granting peace to the soul. Finally, the Muslim is internally reminded after the prayer that the soul is indeed a blessing from God. The true originator and the ultimate source of peace.

As one returns to worldly affairs after prayer, a sense of peace and calmness starts to manifest internally and when amongst people. By engaging in this manner, the Muslim becomes spiritually infectious for those who seek internal nourishment. In this way, God ultimately becomes a source of light and a companion for people throughout their lives in every way. This is the power of prayer in Islam, a constant reflective state of the heart through God's light.

In the next chapter, we explore the connection between *salah* and *Zakah* and how to ensure a healthy balance is maintained between spirituality and materialism.

ZAKAH

Upon establishing an understanding of *salah,* its impact on regulating the heart and its relation to God, attention is now given to another ritual pillar in Islam, namely charity, known in Arabic as '*Zakah'*. *Zakah* has various meanings including 'purification' and 'growth', the notion being that material possessions are purified through monetary donations to those in need. This in turn enables spiritual growth to develop in one's relations with wealth.

What is *Zakah*?

In Islam, *zakah* is an annual form of monetary servitude to God that enables people to benefit from their wealth in various ways. This ritual is binding upon all adults who have the financial capacity to give charity whilst being free from any debt or financial burden, as this will cause monetary harm to oneself and one's family.

Who receives *zakah*?

In terms of who can receive charity, the Quran makes the following statement: **"The alms are only for the poor and the needy, and those who collect them, and those whose hearts are to be reconciled, and to free the captives and the debtors, and for the cause of Allah, and (for) the wayfarers; a duty imposed by Allah. Allah is Knower, Wise"** (*al-Tawbah* 9: 60). Therefore, *zakah* is distributed among eight categories of people, as follows:

a) *Faqeer* – One who has neither material possessions nor any means of livelihood consecutively.

b) *Miskeen* – One with low or insufficient means of moderate livelihood to meet standard needs.

c) *Aamil* – One who has the responsibility to collect *zakah*.

d) *Muallaf* – One who converts to Islam and has no means of support.

e) *Riqaab* – One who frees himself from the shackles of slavery or lack of freedom.

f) *Gharimeen* – One who is in immense debt.

g) *Fee sabeelillah* – One who strives for the cause of God. Within the context of the Quran and its revelatory period, this refers to those that defended Muslim empires from invasion. This is like the financial benefits the armed forces receive by their service to the Queen in the UK.

h) *Ibnus Sabeel* – One who is stranded and lost.

The link between *zakah* and spiritual growth

The act of giving helps regulate one's attitude towards wealth by thanking God for His gifts and sharing it with others selflessly. God states in the Quran: **"My Mercy extends to all things." That (Mercy) I shall ordain for those who have God-consciousness and give their *zakat* and those who believe in Our Signs"** (*al-A'raf* 7:156).

Zakah is considered a means to receive access to the prism of God's love like *salah* and *shahada*. *Zakah* enables the soul to attain freedom from materialism and find solace in God's spiritual sustenance in this world and the hereafter. *Zakah* is therefore a reminder that wealth and sustenance are decreed by God, and nothing is essentially owned by humankind. Rethinking selflessness and materialism in this way creates an enhanced spiritual relationship with God and wealth.

If prayer is to primarily enhance one's connection with God, then *zakah* is a form of spiritual engagement with God's creation through monetary service. This also means creating sustainable wealth through the investment of societal and environmental projects to help the needy.

Expanding charity through the gift of humanity

Besides acts of charity such as the distribution of wealth, charitable acts of humanity and good character are also considered praiseworthy and commended. The Prophet Muhammad (peace and blessings be upon him) emphasised smiling at others and removing harm from people's way as acts of charitable quality. He once said: **"You cannot satisfy people with your wealth but satisfy them with your cheerful faces and upright morals"** (Al-Hakim: 1577), and **"Smiling in your brother's face is an act of charity"** (At-Tirmidhi: 1956). Quite simply, if one has no means of benefitting people through wealth, then enhancing one's integrity and character towards others is always encouraged. This is in no way considered less. To support this point, the Quran numerously
mentions *salah* alongside *zakah,* for various reasons.

Firstly, *salah* enhances the heart and turns it towards positivity, infused with humanity and light. Secondly, *zakah* is an extension of that acquired positivity in that it serves humanity through wealth and traits of selflessness. The greater the amount of habitual prayer during the day and night, the greater the acts of humanity that develop in the form of charity and exemplary character.

When reading the stories of wise men and women in the Quran, one comes to realise their habitual nature of giving charity after prayer. Within books of Muslim history, one explores the nature of the Prophet Muhammad (peace and blessings be upon him) when praying and giving charity to the point of not returning home until wealth was distributed and nothing was left.

Abu Huraira once said regarding the selflessness of the Prophet Muhammad (peace and blessings be upon him): **"By the One in whose hand is my soul, the Messenger of Allah, peace and blessings be upon him, did not satiate his family with wheat bread for three consecutive nights until he departed from this world"** (Muslim: 2976). Such was his selflessness and that of his family in putting other people first. The acquisition of spiritual sustenance had become more meaningful to them than the acquisition of this world. Their goal was to prepare for heavenly bliss with God in the hereafter through attachment to God in this world. By understanding the tradition of the Prophet Muhammad (peace and blessings be upon him) in this manner, one can begin to appreciate the vast difference between spiritual and worldly possessions.

The richness of the heart is greater than all worldly riches. Abu Dharr once said: **"The Messenger of Allah, peace and blessings be upon him, said, 'O Abu Dharr, do you think an abundance of possessions is wealth?' I replied yes. The Prophet asked, 'Do you think a lack of possessions is poverty?' I replied yes. The Prophet repeated this three times, then he said, 'Wealth is in the heart and poverty is in the heart. Whoever is wealthy in his heart will not be harmed no matter what happens in the world. Whoever is impoverished in his heart will not be satisfied no matter how much he has in the world. Verily, he will only be harmed by the greed of his soul'"** (al-Mu'jam al-Kabir: 1618).

Fulfilling the duty of *zakah* is burdensome if the heart is habitually inclined towards the riches of this world. Serving God through selfless charity creates worldly detachment within the heart. Once the heart becomes dematerialised through prayer and charity, the attraction of the material world becomes minimal to the human being. This is then compared to the richness of God's love and spiritual sustenance. Furthermore, one becomes mature and responsible in expenditure and mindful of one's possessions. For example, if one has surplus clothing, money and possessions, voluntary donations can be made to local, national and international charities to benefit the needy. In this manner, everyone has a part to play in the act of charity, even if they have no means to fulfil the annual monetary requirement of *zakah*.

As discussed in the chapter regarding *salah*, it was understood that obtaining peace through prayer benefits one's internal and external affairs. Through the act of *zakah*, if one cannot attain peace within the frame of one's sustenance through acts of charity, then one should revisit prayer and explore the spiritual purpose of life. Attaining peace within the heart can happen once re-evaluation of life takes place habitually.

Materialism is a set of many themes, such as external beauty, ornamentation, positions of worldly power and much more. Charity, in this regard, refers to maintaining a balance between one's loyalty to God and serving the world. This may be very difficult to maintain, as there are times when one can lose focus on one thing or the other. However, by looking at the life of the Prophet Muhammad (peace and blessings be upon him), one comes to know that he enjoyed some of the material world in food, drink, marriage and so on. So, there is no harm in the enjoyment of life but there needs to be a spiritual balance.

Zakah is also considered a way of measuring one's commitment to the world compared to one's commitment to God. When one begins to rely on God throughout life, a particular state of the heart known as *'Tawakkul'* develops. *Tawakkul* refers to having spiritual dependency upon God in all affairs. This state brings immense peace to one's soul and one becomes content with life in general. This can also be considered a key ingredient to attaining a balance between the desire for God and the desire for wealth.

In Islam, charity is considered a means to increase one's decreed sustenance. The Prophet Muhammad (peace and blessings be upon him) once said: **"Charity does not decrease wealth, no one forgives another, but that Allah elevates his honour, and no one humbles himself for the sake of Allah, but that Allah raises his status"** (Muslim: 2588). This means that charity increases contentment and blessings according to God's decree. The Arabic word utilised for blessings is '*Barakah*'. *Barakah* refers to God's spiritual blessings and the attainment of contentment through any amount of wealth, children, food and so on.

Balancing wealth and spirituality

By now, one will have come to understand the immense benefit of charity and its impact on regulating the human condition. The opposite of selflessness is selfishness, which can darken the soul and de-regulate it.

The Prophet Muhammad (peace and blessings be upon him) once forewarned of a time when Muslims would be many in the world but weak in faith and reputation. He said: **"The nations are about to call each other and set upon you, just as diners set upon food." It was posed: "Will it be because of our small number that day?" He answered: "Rather, on that day you will be many, but you will be like foam, like the foam on the river. And Allah will remove the fear of you from the hearts of your enemies and will throw *wahan* (weakness) into your hearts." Someone said: "O Messenger of Allah! What is *wahan*?" He said: "Love of the world and hatred for death"** (Abu Dawud: 4297). He made this statement to emphasise two key matters: love for this world and fear of death. Let us explore this prophetic statement further.

Firstly, the 'weakness of hearts' refers to a lack of spiritual development and discipline which leads to weakness in dependency upon God and ritual performance. Therefore, instead of maintaining a balance between serving God and attaining wealth, one then prefers to balance oneself and wealth instead.

Furthermore, love of the world is also considered the cause of fear of death. 'Fear of death' refers to avoiding the reality of the afterlife, where one will meet God for assessment. Refusing to reflect on one's purpose in life and the afterlife leads to an avoidance in acknowledging the reality of the soul's journey into the afterlife. By being clear about the reality of life and death, the spiritual roadmap towards God becomes meaningful to the individual.

In Islam, death is considered the bridge to the hereafter, rather than an end to all things. This worldly life is indeed part of the soul's journey towards God.

The Quran constantly mentions the reality of life and death. When a Muslim dies, people say the following supplication, which is a verse found in the Quran: **"To God we belong and**

to Him we shall return" (*al-Baqarah* 2: 156). Thereafter, once the deceased is given a ritual wash and shrouded in white cloth they are then buried. Once buried, the soil is sprinkled upon the grave whilst Muslims supplicate using the following Quranic verse: **"We created you from it, and we shall return you into it, and we shall return you from it another time"** (*Ta Ha* 20: 55). Participants in the funeral procession are reminded by this that their moment of death will come one day as well.

In another verse of the Quran, God states: **"Remember that the present life in this world is merely a sport and a pastime; a time when people play foolish games, competing against one another for greater wealth and larger families. The present life is like a plant that flourishes after rain: the gardener is glad to see it grow; but soon it will wither, turning yellow, and become worthless stubble. Success in this world counts for nothing"** (*al-Hadid* 57: 20). This verse clearly states the reality of life and the hereafter, and that the life of this world is indeed a means to prepare for the hereafter. Maintaining spiritual light, receiving spiritual light from others and staying within positive spiritual environments can create a better balance between one's purpose in this life and one's journey towards the hereafter.

To conclude, *zakah* is essentially a means to reform the expenditure of one's wealth and connection to the world through the guidance of the Quran and the Prophet Muhammad (peace and blessings be upon him). This spiritual process begins with a reflective heart in prayer. Prayer in turn activates generosity within the heart. Habitual prayer progressively conditions the relationship between the heart and wealth. Humanity is indeed the greatest form of charity.

In the next chapter, we explore the essence of *Sawm*, another ritual pillar of Islam, through themes of selflessness, patience and gratitude

SAWM

Following on from discussing the spiritual dimensions of
the *shahada, salah* and *zakah,* we now explore another ritual
pillar of Islam, namely *Sawm.*

What is *Sawm*?

Sawm refers to ritual abstention from food, drink and sexual
activities from dawn until sunset. This is commonly
associated with the holy month of Ramadan, the 9th month of
the Islamic calendar. The Islamic calendar consists of twelve
months and is based on the lunar cycle. Each month has either
29 or 30 days. The Quran states: "**Ramadan is the month in
which the Quran was revealed as a guide for humanity
with clear proofs of guidance and the standard to
distinguish between right and wrong. Therefore, whoever
is present this month should fast. But whoever is ill or on a
journey, then let them fast an equal number of days after
Ramadan. Allah intends ease for you, not hardship, so that
you may complete the prescribed period and proclaim the**

greatness of Allah for guiding you, and perhaps you will be grateful" (*al-Baqarah* 2: 181). This verse will be explained in various ways throughout this chapter. The verse makes clear that fasting is prescribed for everyone except those who are either ill, travelling, pregnant or menstruating women. The ease that God speaks of is concerning His devotion. He desires that those who worship Him feel not burdened or troubled by devotional rituals.

The spiritual realm within *sawm* is not just about abstention from food, drink and sexual desires. Rather, *sawm* spiritually recalibrates the relationship between the human heart and carnal desires through repetitive fasting in Ramadan and on other occasions throughout the Islamic year. If the essence of *zakah* is in the detachment of the human heart from negative materialism, *sawm* could then be considered the detachment of the human heart from ill-conceived nourishment through ill-traits such as negative jealousy, hatred, immodesty of character and negative company. The term 'negativity' used here refers to any type of environment or people that can deter one from attaining God's pleasure.

Self-reform and revival in Ramadan

The Prophet Muhammad (peace and blessings be upon him) guaranteed eternal bliss for those who safeguard their speech and body from ill-traits. He said: **"Whoever can guarantee (the chastity of) what is between his two jaw-bones and what is between his two legs (i.e., his tongue and his private parts), I guarantee Paradise for him"** (Bukhari: 6474). This statement is a way to encourage people to speak and act with dignity and modesty. It can also be understood from this statement that paradise refers to a state of internal and external peace in this world and the hereafter.

Being chaste through speech and actions requires much discipline and mindful reflection. *Sawm* offers a chance to redeem oneself through fasting and reflection.

It could be argued that fasting during Ramadan has an immediate impact on the human soul. Therefore, Muslims earnestly help others during Ramadan through charity and humanitarian works, as their hearts are in a process of spiritual change through their fasting.

When Muslims are in a state of fasting, a process of reflection begins to develop through continuous patience throughout the day and gratitude at night once eating is allowed. This continuous state then helps one to achieve gradual control of one's thoughts and desires, instantly soothing the carnal desires of the human heart. In this manner, Muslims become more aware of God's light and presence due to gradual clarity of the mind achieved through intense reflection. In becoming more aware of God's presence throughout the days of fasting, a calmness within the mind, body and soul develops continuously. This is the beauty of Ramadan, in which God's mercy is apparent for all that know Him. It is never too late for one to self-reform.

God's love is with each human being by default. It is up to everyone to embrace Him so that the life of this world forms a premonition to eternal bliss in the hereafter. God's love is considered unlimited in Islam, and that becomes more apparent through fasting habitually. Not only does a state of gratitude and servitude develop, but a sense of belonging to God increases too.

The relationship between the Quran and Ramadan

The Quran is considered to have been revealed in the month of Ramadan. The blessedness of Ramadan is amplified through the regular recital and understanding of the Quran. This means that any sort of connection developed with the Quran during Ramadan can have a lasting impact within the heart. This will enable people to attain clarity of purpose in life. God states in the Quran: **"The Quran was revealed in the month of Ramadan as a guide for mankind"** (*al-Baqarah* 2:185). Understanding the spiritual link between Ramadan and the Quran causes one to seek spiritual guidance through reciting the Quran and applying its wisdom in life.

Fasting is more than just an Islamic tradition

The Quran also highlights that the act of fasting was prescribed for other communities before Islam so that they could become God-conscious and of righteous character. The Quran states: **"Oh you who believe! Fasting is prescribed for you, as it was prescribed for those before you, so that you may become righteous. [The prescribed fasting is] for**

a fixed number of days, but whoso among you is sick or is on a journey [shall fast] the same number on other days; and for those who can fast [only] with significant difficulty, there is an expiation – the feeding of a poor man. Anyone who performs a good work with willing obedience is more fortunate. And fasting is good for you, if only you knew" (*al-Baqarah* 2: 183). Fasting was considered the norm for all of God's chosen prophets so that spiritual discipline was maintained throughout life.

Fasting does not deplete the body of energy but replenishes it with God's light. The Quran is nourishment for the soul in terms of resetting one's relationship with God and mankind. Depending on the receiver's level of attachment to the Quran, it fills the heart with light and healing. Through a combination of fasting and reciting the Quran during Ramadan, elements of modesty are adopted in life. In this manner, the Muslim finds a return to ill-character much more difficult post-Ramadan.

Modesty in Islam

The common word used in Islam regarding modesty is '*Hayaa*' although some would argue that the Arabic term *hayaa* encompasses much more meaning than simply the term 'modesty'. This will be explored further ahead.

Urrah ibn Iyas once said: **"We were with the Messenger of Allah (peace and blessings be upon him) when the topic of modesty was mentioned to him. They inquired, 'O Messenger of Allah, is modesty part of the religion?' The Prophet said, 'Rather, it is the entire religion.' Then, the Prophet said, 'Verily, modesty, abstinence, the reticence of the tongue and the heart, and deeds are all part of faith. They bring gain in the Hereafter and loss in the world: what is gained in the Hereafter is much greater than what is missed in the world"** (Sunan al-Kubra: 20808).

Hayaa is essentially the honouring of the human soul by maintaining spiritual dignity in noble work and character. If *hayaa* is primarily interpreted as an outlook to symbolise God's subservience through clothing and worldly status, traits such as vanity, flair and pomp are then seen as the hallmark of the uncultured soul. When *hayaa* is implemented from a place of inward reflection, stemming from a regulated heart driven by a level of God-consciousness, it then becomes meaningful and spiritually long-lasting in one's character. Fasting boosts the process of inward reflection if done in the right manner through the implementation of character-driven *hayaa* during

Ramadan. Therefore, besides just fasting from dawn until sunset, the benefit of fasting primarily lies within the *hayaa* of noble character and spiritual growth.

The Prophet Muhammad (peace and blessings be upon him) said concerning this: **"Verily, every religion has a character, and the character of Islam is modesty"** (Sunan Ibn Majah: 4182). Furthermore, the Prophet Muhammad (peace and blessings be upon him) likened one's righteous character to the virtues of fasting. He said: **"Verily, the believer may reach by his righteous character the rank of one who regularly fasts and stands for prayer at night"** (Sunan Abu Dawud: 4798). This does not negate the ritual of fasting. The prophet Muhammad (peace and blessings upon him) encourages those who fast to also ensure that they maintain their character at the same time to attain the benefits of both worlds. Furthermore, *hayaa* increases with righteous character to the point that one attains a reflective state through prayer and fasting.

The Prophet Muhammad (peace and blessings be upon him) also explained that the gates of heaven are open during Ramadan. This means that those who maintain spiritual discipline through fasting enjoy the sweetness of faith and enjoy the realm of God's grace in this world and the afterlife.

Besides spiritually benefitting from fasting in Ramadan, the human body also benefits through physical detox and increased positive levels of health. As a result of combining the spiritual and physical benefits of fasting, the mind improves as well as motivation in life. Hence, through fasting, the Muslim becomes naturally drawn to prayer and the search for meaning in life. Therefore, one will notice many Muslims who become more pious and practice faith during Ramadan than at other times of the year.

The experience of reforming the soul through fasting and prayer ends with the occasion of Eid, which marks the end of Ramadan. The communal joy experienced at Eid is indeed a celebration of purified souls joined together by God through prayer, festivities and love.

Whether fasting is practised during Ramadan or beyond, the spiritual benefits of it, as explored above, are always there to gain. Like all other rituals in Islam, *sawm* is truly a devotional act that intensifies one's relationship with God.

The beneficial outcome of fasting reflects the intention of the fasting individual. In Islam, having clarity of purpose and intention is key to establishing the long-term benefits of rituals. The positivity that comes with such rituals in turn remains long-lasting and enjoyable.

To conclude, *sawm* is an integral part of reviving the human soul and a unique way to fill the emptiness of the heart with God's light.

HAJ

After understanding the spiritual dimensions of the
shahada, *salah*, *zakah* and *sawm*, we now come to explore the
final ritual pillar in Islam known as *Haj*.

What is *Haj*?

Haj refers to the pilgrimage or holy journey to Makkah and
Madinah for a set number of days during the Islamic month
of *Zul-Hijjah*. During the pilgrimage, rituals are performed by
Muslims that emulate the Prophet Abraham[4] and Prophet
Muhammad (peace be upon them) such as walking to specific
sites, drinking holy water, praying, performing an animal
sacrifice and much more. God states in the Quran **"*Haj* shall
be observed in the specified months. Whoever sets out to**

---

[4] Abraham (peace be upon him) is commonly considered the
founder of three monotheistic faiths: Judaism, Christianity and
Islam. Within Islam, he holds special reverence due to his close
relationship with God and as such, he is considered in Islam as the
friend of God.

observe *haj* shall refrain from sexual intercourse, misconduct, and arguments throughout *haj*. Whatever goodness you do, God is fully aware thereof. As you prepare your provisions for the journey, the most beneficial provision is righteousness. You shall observe Me, O you who possess intelligence" (*al-Baqarah* 2: 197).

Haj is considered obligatory for those that can afford to travel and are healthy. This does not mean that the spiritual blessings of *haj* are exclusive to pilgrims to Makkah and Madinah only. Rather, during the month of *haj*, both pilgrims and non-pilgrims can benefit from the spirit of *haj*. This will be explored later in this chapter.

The concept of pilgrimage also lies within other faith traditions besides Islam including Christianity, Buddhism and Hinduism. In each of these faith traditions, many sacred centres have been developed as focal points for adherents to make specific journeys to reinvigorate their faith. It is not only in major religious traditions that pilgrimage is considered a key concept. This is because it is also prevalent in traditions that are connected to cultures and ethnicities such as the Shinto tradition in Japan.

The concept of establishing devotion to God through constant reflection as one spiritual body is fundamental to the purpose of the pilgrimage. During the pilgrimage, a special attire is worn by pilgrims named *Ihram*. *Ihram* refers to two pieces of unsewn white cloth wrapped around the upper and lower body during the pilgrimage. The reason for this simple form of attire during *haj* is to highlight the equality of all pilgrims in the court of God. It is also a reminder to pilgrims of the reality of death and the afterlife, where riches will turn to rags and flesh to bones. Furthermore, this displays the importance of spiritual purity besides external appearances when it comes to serving God.

The Prophet Muhammad (peace and blessing be upon him) said: **"God looks not at your appearance nor wealth but at your heart and actions"** (Muslim: 2564). This indicates the importance of internal wholeness, spiritual growth and good character. If *shahada* is a means to testify to the greatness of God in this world, then *haj* is to testify to the greatness of God in the afterlife through its arduous journey. The journey to Makkah and Madinah is indeed a way of redirecting the reflective soul towards the reality of life and death.

Besides visiting Makkah and Madinah, we experience the concept of pilgrimage every day when we interact with family members and friends. We are all pilgrims to one another and towards our daily goals. *Haj* is a way of highlighting the essence of what it means to be the greatest pilgrim in life, a pilgrim of God. The desire to connect with God to receive His grace gradually happens by devoting time to Him as a pilgrim every day.

The Ka'bah

Mosques are established to become beacons of spirituality within Muslim communities. However, the greatest mosque is the one located in Makkah, the Grand Mosque. When Muslims visit Makkah, they visit the Grand Mosque. There, they come across a tall building draped with a black cloth known as the Ka'bah situated at the epicentre of the Grand Mosque.

What is the significance of this building?

This building is made from bricks and stones and was renovated by the Prophet Abraham and his son Ishmael (peace be upon them) after it had been damaged by floods throughout many centuries. God states in the Quran: **"We have rendered the shrine (the Ka'bah) a focal point for the people, and a** safe sanctuary. You may use Abraham's shrine as a prayer house. We commissioned Abraham and Ismail: "You shall purify My house for those who visit, those who live there, and those who bow and prostrate" (*al-Baqarah* 2: 125).

In Islam, it is understood that the Prophet Adam (peace be upon him), considered the first man on earth, had originally built the Ka'bah to call people towards it for God's worship. After it had been built, a special stone from heaven, now known as 'the black stone ', was gifted by God for placement near the Ka'bah. This stone is considered to emancipate everyone that encounters it by giving hope for redemption and revival of the soul.

Travelling around the Ka'bah

The Islamic concept of circulating the Ka'bah during *haj* is to highlight the circulation of God within our souls when we devote ourselves to Him. Similarly, celestial bodies, animals, things we can see and cannot are all circulating in their way around God metaphysically. God states in the Quran: **"And it is He Who created the night and the day, and the sun and the moon. They float, each in an orbit"** (*al-Anbiya'* 21: 33).

From a theological point of view in Islam, this denotes the devotion of God's creation towards Him.

The Ka'bah symbolises the Oneness of God in that all within the heavens and the earth circulates to His will naturally. Though each human being is continuously in the process of being a pilgrim in life, the greatest pilgrimage is to God. And that is the essence of spiritual fulfilment; at peace within one's heart.

During *haj*, visits to various holy sites are carried out by pilgrims, such as the hills of *Safa* and *Mar*wa and visiting the tomb[5] of the Prophet Muhammad (peace and blessing be upon him). God states in the Quran: **"Lo! (The mountains) *As-Safa* and *Al-Marwa* are among the indications of Allah. It is therefore no sin for him who is on pilgrimage to the House (of Allah) or visits it, to wander around them (as the pagan custom is). And he who does right of his own accord, (for him) lo! Allah is Responsive, Aware"** (*al-Baqarah* 2:158).

---

[5] Islamic scholars have said, "Visiting the blessed shrine of the Holy Prophet Muhammad (peace be upon him) is a means of the perfection of *Haj*" (Fayz-ul-Qadeer, 8716).

The prophet Muhammad said: **"On the Day of Judgement, I will be the intercessor or witness of the one who visits my grave. And the one who dies in any of the holy sites (Makah and Madinah) will be resurrected by Allah among those granted peace"** (Sunan Kubra lil-Bayhaqi, 10273).

Symbolism is a prominent feature within Islam concerning clothing, structures and art. These are all expressions of interpreting devotion to God in a way that broadens the path to His pleasure.

When one travels to Makkah and Madinah and hears the chant of 'Allahu Akbar, God is Mighty,' the soul resonates within one's heart. This causes a state of reflection and awareness to develop. It is in this state that pilgrims, upon witnessing the Ka'bah for the first time, have an outpouring of emotion and love for God. Those pilgrims who have been to visit the holy sites know well what this feeling entails and how it purifies the heart.

Whilst staying in Makkah, the heart becomes drawn to the Ka'bah like a magnet. The heart is also drawn to visiting the tomb of the Prophet Muhammad (peace and blessings be upon him) in Madinah to pay respects in a state of profound emotion. An internal state of spiritual renewal and emotional outpouring is essentially the outcome of maintaining the *haj* tradition throughout life. This also ties in with the other spiritual pillars of Islam through the process of spiritual recalibration of the heart, mind and body towards God.

Why do Muslims revere Muhammad (peace and blessings be upon him)?

Muslims honour the Prophet Muhammad (peace and blessings be upon him) throughout their lives. Visiting Madinah during the pilgrimage is one form of paying respect to him. Other forms of showing respect to him include emulating his way of life in every way and praising him upon his remembrance.

The Arabic term used for this praise is '*Salaat wa Salam*', which translates as 'peace and blessings'. The most common form of verbal honour to the Prophet Muhammad is '*Sal-lal-lahu alay- he- wa-sal-lam*', which means 'peace and blessings of Allah be upon him.'

The Prophet Muhammad (peace and blessing be upon him) is considered God's Mercy to mankind, hence, his mission was to portray the love of God to everyone. God states in the

Quran: **"We sent you not but as a mercy for the worlds"** (*al-Anbiya* '21: 107).

In Islam, the Prophet Muhammad (peace and blessings be upon him) is the culmination of all of God's prophets. His mission was like that of other prophets in that he taught mankind about the Oneness of God and the importance of service to humanity.

The Prophet Muhammad (peace and blessings be upon him) grew up as an orphan, lived for 63 years and lived a simple life of honour, justice and love. He was conscious of differences among people and wished to address issues of petty rivalry and transgression within his community in 7th century Arabia.

To broadly understand this further in the context of this chapter, we look at the Prophet Muhammad's (peace and blessings be upon him) final sermon, delivered during *haj* on mount Arafah in Makkah. This sermon was pivotal in the longevity of his spiritual community and primarily addresses the fact that God's light is equal for all. In the sermon many issues were raised, but here are some of the key points:

a) The rights of orphans and widows were to be mandated and fulfilled permanently.

b) Assurance of the equality of people regardless of colour or background.

c) Fulfilling the rights of women in every way.

These issues were troubling matters in his lifetime, and he sought to eradicate injustices and enhance the rights of everyone by aligning himself with community activists throughout his life.

Concerning equality of life through love and harmony, the Quran states: **"Oh mankind, indeed we have created you in pairs, male and female, and into tribes and nations so that you recognise each other. Indeed, the most honourable to God are those who attain God-consciousness. Indeed, He is all-knowing and all-aware"** (*al-Hujurat* 49: 13). This verse sets out the reality of life and the fact that all are equal. The idea of recognition amongst people here is to appreciate differences in faith, colour and background. The idea of honour within this verse lies within the realm of respect, love and exemplary character. The Quran then states that the essence of ensuring lasting values of respect, love and good character lies within the traits of God-consciousness.

By understanding the verse in alignment with the final sermon of the Prophet Muhammad (peace and blessings be upon him) during *haj*, a call to diverse unity and plurality is understood to be an integral part of the Muslim tradition. Therefore, engaging with people through a mode of Islamic pluralism becomes an essential part of what it means to be a Muslim. Islamic pluralism is arguably a contentious issue for some Muslims due to the societal complexities surrounding migration, security of faith, lack of coherent theological development and community engagement. This significant matter is to be explored at another time.

A Muslim is at peace with God and mankind through a state of constant purity within the heart, mind and body. A Muslim is the embodiment of peace, love and justice. Muslims must keep people safe as much as themselves so that humankind can share in the love of God in every way.

CONCLUSION

This book has focused entirely on the journey of the human soul through exploration of the five spiritual pillars of Islam. The spiritual journey to God through the implementation of these pillars is never-ending. These pillars are indeed significant milestones for exploring Islamic spirituality in any capacity of time and space.

The Prophet Muhammad (peace and blessing be upon him) once said: **"Actions are judged by their intentions"** (Bukhari: 54). Whatever intention one holds whilst undertaking these spiritual pillars will reflect outcomes in this world and the hereafter.

Besides having a purposeful intention to commit to God, it is also imperative to inculcate a state of *Muhasabah* daily. *Muhasabah* is essentially journaling one's life through daily reflection, thought and practice. Muslim scholars throughout the centuries have always encouraged daily journaling as a way of keeping the mind occupied with religious motivation and spiritual fulfilment. The power of intention maintained in this manner develops a gradual construct of inner ascendency whilst performing rituals. In each moment of progress, paying attention to one's intention before each Islamic ritual results in beneficial outcomes.

It is not the quantity of each action that holds virtue in Islam but its spiritual quality. In Islam, a higher level of spiritual quality in one's heart towards God during rituals is considered more fulfilling. Every path to God carries profound value and should not be undermined through lack of quantity in devotion.

In Islam, God's love for humankind has always been there, even before the creation of the universe and its entities. His love encompasses everything within us and around us. He sees us and knows our yearning for everlasting peace. His door is always open for those that wish to seek light amid the darkness. The pillars of Islam are paths towards achieving spiritual enlightenment. Indeed, God is light, and He shines within the universe and beyond.

When one is mindful of one's place in the world with purpose, the heart is sealed with the blessings of *shahada*. The heart is sealed with the blessings of *salah* when one is aware of its benefits and practices it during the day and at night. Whenever one is selfless and strives to serve humanity, the heart is sealed with the blessings of *zakah*. When one fasts with body and spiritual mindfulness, the heart is sealed with the blessings of *sawm*. And lastly, when one directs themselves to God in life, the heart is sealed with the blessings of *haj*. All of this, in turn, activates five established paths of spiritual healing towards God.

May this book motivate you to become an embodiment of God's light on earth so that others are illuminated through your glowing soul.

May God's peace and blessings be with us all. Ameen.

99 NAMES AND ATTRIBUTES OF ALLAH

Besides acknowledging Allah for His majestic and glorious position as the originator of all things known and unknown to the world, there are other attributes of Allah that diversify one's understanding of Him and our cosmic reality in space and time. The Qur'an states:

"He is Allah, the Creator, the Inventor, the Fashioner; to Him belong the most honorable names. Whatever is in the heavens and earth exalts Him. And He is the Exalted in Might, the Wise" (*al-Hashr* 59:24).

"And to Allah belong the best names, so invoke Him by them" (*al-A 'raf* 7:180).

"Allah – there is no deity except Him. To Him belong the most excellent names" (*Ta Ha* 20:8).

Muslims are encouraged to call upon Allah through His attributes, termed the '99 names'. In doing so, the human being connects with God when engaged in prayers and remembrance in the meaning of life and death.

The Prophet Muhammad (peace and blessings be upon him) once said, **"Allah has ninety-nine names, and whoever knows them will be taken to Paradise"** (Bukhari, 894).

The link between knowing Allah's 99 names and gaining entrance to paradise is based on enhancing one's soul through engaging with Allah's multi-dimensional light in a manner that grants peace and serenity within the heart. In other words, the true essence of paradise is achieved when the soul is filled with the love of Allah and illuminated by intense recognition of His attributes. The paradise of the hereafter and its luxuries are not equal to the paradise of Allah's pleasure.

Further ahead is a chart displaying Allah's 99 Arabic names in English transliteration with their meaning. The English language cannot do justice to the density of the Arabic language, and the Arabic language cannot do justice to interpreting Allah and His majestic attributes. We will, however, suffice with our human understanding of language and interpretation as per Allah's wisdom.

#	Name	Meaning
1	**AR-RAHMAAN**	The Beneficent
2	**AR-RAHEEM**	The Merciful
3	**AL-MALIK**	The Eternal Lord
4	**AL-QUDDUS**	The Most Sacred
5	**AS-SALAM**	The Embodiment of Peace
6	**AL-MU'MIN**	The Infuser of Faith
7	**AL-MUHAYMIN**	The Preserver of Safety
8	**AL-AZIZ**	The All-Mighty
9	**AL-JABBAR**	The Compeller, The Restorer
10	**AL-MUTAKABBIR**	The Supreme, The Majestic
11	**AL-KHAALIQ**	The Creator, The Maker
12	**AL-BAARI**	The Evolver
13	**AL-MUSAWWIR**	The Fashioner
14	**AL-GHAFFAR**	The Great Forgiver
15	**AL-QAHHAR**	The All-Prevailing One
16	**AL-WAHHAAB**	The Supreme Bestower
17	**AR-RAZZAAQ**	The Provider
18	**AL-FATTAAH**	The Supreme Solver
19	**AL-'ALEEM**	The All-Knowing
20	**AL-QAABID**	The Withholder

21	**AL-BAASIT**	The Extender
22	**AL-KHAAFIDH**	The Reducer
23	**AR-RAAFI'**	The Exalter, The Elevator
24	**AL-MU'IZZ**	The Honourer, The Bestower
25	**AL-MUZIL**	The Dishonourer, The Humiliator
26	**AS-SAMEE'**	The All-Hearing
27	**AL-BASEER**	The All-Seeing
28	**AL-HAKAM**	The Impartial Judge
29	**AL-'ADL**	The Utterly Just
30	**AL-LATEEF**	The Subtle One, The Gentlest
31	**AL-KHABEER**	The All-Aware
32	**AL-HALEEM**	The Most Forbearing
33	**AL-'AZEEM**	The Magnificent, The Supreme
34	**AL-GHAFOOR**	The Great Forgiver
35	**ASH-SHAKOOR**	The Most Appreciative
36	**AL-'ALEE**	The Highest, The Exalted
37	**AL-KABEER**	The Preserver, The All-Heedful and All-Protecting
38	**AL-HAFEEDH**	The Preserver
39	**AL-MUQEET**	The Sustainer
40	**AL-HASEEB**	The Reckoner
41	**AL-JALEEL**	The Majestic
42	**AL-KAREEM**	The Most Generous, The Most Esteemed

43	AR-RAQEEB	The Watchful
44	AL-MUJEEB	The Responsive One
45	AL-WAASI'	The All-Encompassing, The Boundless
46	AL-HAKEEM	The All-Wise
47	AL-WADUD	The Most Loving
48	AL-MAJEED	The Glorious, The Most Honourable
49	AL-BA'ITH	The Infuser of New Life
50	ASH-SHAHEED	The All-Observing Witnessing
51	AL-HAQQ	The Absolute Truth
52	AL-WAKEEL	The Trustee, The Disposer of Affairs
53	AL-QAWIYY	The All-Strong
54	AL-MATEEN	The Firm, The Steadfast
55	AL-WALIYY	The Protecting Associate
56	AL-HAMEED	The Praiseworthy
57	AL-MUHSEE	The All-Enumerating, The Counter
58	AL-MUBDI	The Originator, The Initiator
59	AL-MUEED	The Restorer, The Reinstater
60	AL-MUHYI	The Giver of Life
61	AL-MUMEET	The Inflicter of Death
62	AL-HAYY	The Ever-Living
63	AL-QAYYOOM	The Sustainer, The Self-Subsisting

64	**AL-WAAJID**	The Perceiver
65	**AL-MAAJID**	The Illustrious, The Magnificent
66	**AL-WAAHID**	The One
67	**AL-AHAD**	The Unique, The Only One
68	**AS-SAMAD**	The Eternal, The Satisfier of Needs
69	**AL-QADEER**	The Omnipotent One
70	**AL-MUQTADIR**	The Powerful
71	**AL-MUQADDIM**	The Expediter, The Promoter
72	**AL-MU'AKHKHIR**	The Delayer
73	**AL-AWWAL**	The First
74	**AL-AAKHIR**	The Last
75	**AZ-ZAAHIR**	The Manifest
76	**AL-BAATIN**	The Hidden One, The Knower of the Hidden
77	**AL-WAALI**	The Governor, The Patron
78	**AL-MUTA'ALI**	The Self Exalted
79	**AL-BARR**	The Source of All Goodness
80	**AT-TAWWAB**	The Ever-Pardoning, The Relenting
81	**AL-MUNTAQIM**	The Avenger
82	**AL-'AFUWW**	The Pardoner

83	**AR-RA'OOF**	The Most Kind
84	**MAALIK-UL-MULK**	Master of the Kingdom, Owner of the Dominion
85	**DHUL-JALAALI-WAL-IKRAAM**	Possessor of Glory and Honour, Lord of Majesty and Generosity
86	**AL-MUQSIT**	The Just One
87	**AL-JAAMI'**	The Gatherer, The Uniter
88	**AL-GHANIYY**	The Self-Sufficient, The Wealthy
89	**AL-MUGHNI**	The Enricher
90	**AL-MANI'**	The Withholder
91	**AD-DHARR**	The Distresser
92	**AN-NAFI'**	The Propitious, The Benefactor
93	**AN-NUR**	The Light, The Illuminator
94	**AL-HAADI**	The Guide
95	**AL-BADEE'**	The Incomparable Originator
96	**AL-BAAQI**	The Everlasting
97	**AL-WAARITH**	The Inheritor, The Heir
98	**AR-RASHEED**	The Guide, The Infallible Teacher
99	**AS-SABOOR**	The Forbearing, The Patient

NOTES

GLOSSARY

Allah – God

Allahu Akbar - God is Almighty

Haj - the Muslim pilgrimage

Hayaa - modesty

Iman - faith

Ka'bah – the name of God's house in Makkah

Madinah – a city in present day Saudi Arabia

Makkah – a city in present day Saudi Arabia

Muhasabah - reflection

Nafs - the 'self' or inner voice

Qalb – the human heart

Ruh – the human soul

Salah – prayer

Salat and salam - peace and blessings

Sallallahu alayhi wasallam – peace and blessings of
Allah be upon him

Sawm - fasting

Shahada – testification

Wudu - ablution

Zakat – the annual Muslim charity

BIBLIOGRAPHY

Ali, A. (1953), *The Spirit of Islam*, Lulu. Com.

Al-Karam, C. Y. (2018), "Islamic Psychology: Towards a 21st century definition and conceptual framework", *Journal of Islamic Ethics*, 2(1-2), 97-109.

Ashy, M. A. (1999), "Health and Illness from an Islamic Perspective", *Journal of Religion and Health*, 38(3), 241-258

El-Zein, A. (2009), *Islam, Arabs and the Intelligent World of the Jinn*, Syracuse University Press.

Haque, A., Khan, F., Keshavarzi, H. and Rothman, A. E. (2016), "Integrating Islamic Traditions in Modern Psychology: Research trends in last ten years", *Journal of Muslim Mental Health*, 10(1).

Lee, M. T., Poloma, M. M. and Post, S. G. (2013), *The Heart of Religion: Spiritual empowerment, benevolence, and the experience of God's love*, Oxford University Press.

Mourad, S. A. (2019), *The Shahada and the Creation of an Islamic Identity*. In *Geneses* (pp. 218-239). Routledge.

Oliver, E. D. and Lewis, J. R. (2008), *Angels A to Z*, Visible Ink Press.

Rogerson, B. (2010), *The Prophet Muhammad: a biography*, Hachette UK.

Von Stosch, K. (2015), "Does Allah Translate 'God'? Translating Concepts between Religions", *Translating Religion: What is lost and gained*, 47, 123.

Vatikiotis, P. J. (1986), "Between Arabism and Islam", *Middle Eastern Studies*, 22(4), 576-586.

ABOUT THIS BOOK

Many books have been written about the pillars of Islam for both Muslims and non-Muslims that explore themes such as the testimony of faith, prayer, charity, fasting and pilgrimage. Some books have focused on the 'do's and don'ts' of Islam and some have leaned towards facts and figures about Islam and Muslims worldwide. However, it is rare to find a book that explores the psycho-spiritual reasoning behind the five pillars of Islam.

This concise book aims to engage with readers of all backgrounds who are interested in exploring Islam through the lens of spirituality. Exploring Islam in this manner enables the reader to appreciate and understand the spiritual values of Islam and why Muslims adhere to the faith as a way of life.

ABOUT THE AUTHOR

The author, Mohammed Roziur Rahman, was inspired to write this book by Muslim and non-Muslim friends, clients and peers during his 20-year career as a chaplain, Imam and peace activist, working both nationally and internationally. He is an award-winning Imam who has been recognised in the UK for services to dialogue, religious advocacy and community peace building initiatives.

Mohammed Roziur Rahman has been featured on the BBC, ITV and other media platforms discussing issues around mental health, spirituality and community matters. He is preparing further books to be published on topics such as mental health in Muslim communities, poetry, his autobiography and much more.

Printed in Great Britain
by Amazon

27221235R00066